DATE DUE

The PEDDLERS

COLONIAL CRAFTSMEN

The
PEDDLERS

WRITTEN & ILLUSTRATED BY

Leonard Everett Fisher

BENCHMARK BOOKS

MARSHALL CAVENDISH
NEW YORK

Benchmark Books
Marshall Cavendish Corporation
99 White Plains Road
Tarrytown, New York 10591

Copyright © 1968 by Leonard Everett Fisher

First Marshall Cavendish edition 1998

━━━━━━━━━━

Library of Congress Cataloging-in-Publication Data
Fisher, Leonard Everett.
The peddlers / written & illustrated by Leonard Everett Fisher.
p.   cm. — (Colonial craftsmen)
Originally published: New York : F. Watts, 1968
Includes index.
Summary: Describes the enterprise and commercial development that peddlers
brought to the colonies before the establishment of general stores.
ISBN 0-7614-0511-9
1. Peddlers and peddling—United States—Juvenile literature. [1. Peddlers and
peddling. 2. United States—History—Colonial period, ca. 1600–1775.]
I. Title. II. Series: Fisher, Leonard Everett. Colonial craftsmen.
HF5459.U6F4   1998   381'.1—DC20   96-38412   CIP   AC

━━━━━━━━━━

Printed and bound in the United States of America
5   6   4

Other titles in this series
==========

THE CABINETMAKERS
THE DOCTORS
THE GLASSMAKERS
THE HOMEMAKERS
THE SCHOOLMASTERS
THE SHIPBUILDERS
THE SHOEMAKERS
THE SILVERSMITHS
THE WEAVERS

==========

I N THE 1660'S, BOSTON, IN ENGLAND'S colony of Massachusetts, was a busy place. The whole town, with its three thousand Puritan inhabitants, was crowded onto a small peninsula that reached northward into the bay. At its southerly end, Boston was connected to the rest of America by a slim strip of land called Boston Neck. It was hardly wide enough for a footpath. The town's gray-brown, unpainted houses stood on crooked, unpaved streets that twisted around the hills like tangled strings. But cramped and drab as it might look, Boston in the 1660's and for most of the Colonial period was an important seaport — the gateway to America. In the good sailing months there were always ships at its wharves, and sailors roamed through the streets. With each arriving vessel came new colonists, and cargoes of much needed goods for the little settlements in the New World. And sailing with the vessels back to England went loads of lumber, pitch, and furs — raw materials to add to the mother country's wealth.

All day long there was noise and confusion and

coming and going along the Boston docks. Men worked endlessly, bent double under the cargoes that were being unloaded, and the piles of goods on the wharves grew higher. But, even so, there were not enough supplies to fill the needs of the fast-growing colonies in America. Sometimes English ships seemed to take out more things than they brought in.

Moreover, various English laws hindered the trade of the colonies. There were some materials that the colonists were permitted to sell only to England. Many of the American cargoes had to be shipped only to the mother country and paid for with English goods or letters of credit, rather than with hard cash. This trade arrangement was good for England, but because of it many things, including money, were in short supply in the American colonies.

True, some British coins trickled in. Moreover, Bostonian merchants had a lively trade with the West Indies in some things, and through this, many Spanish coins came into the colony. Then too, no handier smugglers ever lived than the shrewd Puritan shipmasters of Boston. They

found ways of slipping in a great many trade goods behind the backs of the British. Still, many of the little things needed for daily living were scarce, and so was money.

In 1652, the people of the Massachusetts colony had taken matters into their own hands and had set up a mint to coin shillings for their own use. Since most of these coins bore the impression of a pine tree, they came to be known as pine tree shillings, though there were some oak and willow tree shillings too. These coins helped the money problem, but still it was difficult.

Difficult, too, for some of the young men of the colony, was the question of a life work. Of course, if a young man had a wealthy father, he might be given the education necessary to become a lawyer or a clergyman or a doctor. Or, if the family owned a business, a son could expect to be taken into that. But the ordinary poor young man had no such choice. He could always go to sea, but seafaring was a hard life with no sure promise for the future. Farming was another way to earn a living, but not all young men cared for it. There were various skilled crafts, too — tailoring or sil-

Pine tree shilling

Pine tree
sixpence

Oak tree shilling

Oak tree
twopence

Willow tree shilling

Willow tree
threepence

versmithing, for instance — but seven years of hard work as an apprentice were needed before a man could set up his own business. There seemed to be little chance for a poor young man to get ahead quickly.

But Boston was full of lively, ambitious young men who kept their eyes open and their minds alert. Some of them were Bostonians; some were English sailors. Both groups knew of the lack of money and of the many shortages of goods. Some of the scarce items seemed fairly unimportant — combs, for example, or needles, or buttons. Unimportant they might sound, but they were necessary, and people found it hard to get along without them. There were many would-be buyers anxious for these goods. Surely there must be some way to supply them and make a little profit too.

There was a way. These items were small in size. How easy it would be for an English sailor to fill a sack of such things before leaving his home port! And what a ready chance for trading them he would have in Boston! Best of all, there was no English law against such dealings.

Now, more closely than ever, the townspeople watched the harbor for approaching ships. Even before a vessel dropped anchor, a swarm of young Bostonians crowded the docks, waiting for the sailors to come ashore. Then, as the seamen opened their bags and showed their wares, the bargaining began. Pots, pans, pins, ribbons, bows, needles, combs, and dozens of other little things — there was a ready market for them all. The sailors had no firm prices. They settled for as much as they could possibly get. If the buyer could pay in money, so much the better. If not, perhaps some trade or barter could be arranged.

The young Bostonians bought whatever they could afford, then headed for the town. From door to door they went, offering their precious goods. The prices they asked were outrageous, but the things they sold were badly needed. A woman could be counted on to give a good sum for a needle or a comb if she had none at all and there was no other way of getting it.

There were no general stores in those days. The only way of buying some kinds of goods was through a peddler. Peddling became a new trade,

and soon some of the young men in the business were on the way to becoming rich and important.

Before long, the streets of Boston became so crowded with these new tradesmen knocking on every door that for a time there seemed to be more peddlers than there were doors. Plainly there was not enough room in Boston for all the would-be peddlers. But to the north was Salem, to the southeast was Plymouth, and beyond them the trails led to other settlements.

Soon some of the first peddlers stopped peddling altogether. They became importers. They bought their goods from the sailors on the wharves, as usual, but they hired other men to do the door-to-door selling. More often than not, these new importers would simply sell a large number of combs, pots, or brass buttons to a peddler. This man would pack them in a bag, sling the bag across his back, cross Boston Neck, and head for the open spaces beyond.

No matter in what direction he chose to go, the peddler walked all the way. His was not an easy stroll that could be taken in a day's time. Plymouth lay about forty-five miles to the south,

and Salem about fifteen miles to the north. No roads led to them, but only trails, hot and dusty and swarming with insects in summer; thick with mud in rainy weather; hard and icy in winter. Nothing could stop the peddlers, however. Soon so many of them filled the trails between Boston, Plymouth, and Salem that they seemed almost like an army on the move. In a way, they were — an army of door-to-door salesmen bringing small, useful articles and housewares to grateful buyers, wherever they lived.

The American colonies were growing rapidly. By 1700, ten thousand people lived in Boston. Thousands upon thousands more lived in large towns, small settlements, and lonely farmhouses from Maine to Georgia. All these people needed many of the articles that were used in daily living. The peddlers were the only persons determined enough to bring them to the customers.

No particular experience was necessary for peddling. Of course, a peddler had to have a good head for business and for driving a sharp bargain. And he needed a strong back and good muscular arms in order to carry his goods. He had to have

sturdy legs for walking long distances. He had to be able to find his way in the wilderness without getting lost, robbed, or attacked by hostile Indians. And he had to guard against poisonous snakes, wild animals, frostbite, or drowning in a desolate, misty swamp. Often he carried his food with him, and slept under the open sky at night. Peddling was no work for a person who was easily frightened. It was a mean job. But a strong and fearless man who wanted to be his own boss might welcome this chance to make a start in business.

Dreaming of riches and adventure, the peddler prepared for his journey by stocking up on those everyday items that few settlers had and that none could do without. Such things as pots, pans, dishes of all sizes and shapes, axes, tools, nails, pins, and buttons were fast sellers. But the biggest profits were to be made on such luxury items as spices, coffee, tea, combs, mirrors, sweet-smelling toilet water, fancy lace, and colorful ribbons. The peddler made sure that he had a supply of as many of these things as he could carry and could afford to buy.

When all his goods were gathered, he packed

them carefully in a long, narrow tin trunk. Small dishes were placed in larger dishes; small pans in larger pans. Small articles like pins and buttons were put in the pots. Delicate laces were placed on less delicate cloth, and together they were rolled around any long object that the peddler might be taking along. When everything was properly packed, the peddler closed the lid securely, hoisted onto his back the trunk — now weighing about fifty pounds — and set out on a selling trip that would keep him away from home for weeks or months.

If he was a very strong fellow, he would also carry a smaller trunk filled with goods. If he could, he bought a horse to carry his heavy load and take him on his way. But horses were scarce during the early Colonial years. The chances were that even if the peddler was able to find such an animal for sale, he could not afford to buy it, especially if he was just starting out on his new career. He usually put every shilling and threepence he had into his stock. Rather than leave the tiniest button out of his trunk, he preferred to walk.

It is a wonder that the peddlers were able to travel as they did. During most of the pre-Revolutionary days in America there were few passable roads between the lonely farmhouses, settlements, villages, or cities. Here and there a person could find good paths and old Indian trails if he knew where to look, and there were some routes that could be followed for long distances. One such route, established between Boston and New York in the 1670's, could hardly be called a first-class road, although it soon became known as the Boston Post Road.

Hacked out of the woodlands, it was a path blocked by streams and rivers at some points and passing through sleepy villages at others. It was a route that scrambled up stony hills thick with brambles and fell away into forested river valleys below. It was there one day and gone the next as it was flooded by rain and swollen rivers, buried under ice or new-fallen snow, or hidden by the fast-growing underbrush. One horseman, traveling almost continuously with the mail, needed almost two weeks to go from New York to Boston. There were times when he could not be sure

whether he was going east, west, north, or south, or whether he was actually on the road at all.

The Boston Post Road had, in fact, three routes: the Upper, Middle, and Lower roads. The Upper Road led from Boston in a southwesterly direction through Springfield and Hartford, to New Haven. The Middle Road followed a very old trail just south of the Upper Road and joined it at Hartford. The Lower Road passed through Providence, Rhode Island, and ran along the shoreline, joining the Upper-Middle Road at New Haven, Connecticut. From there, the road ran on to New York. In 1704, an ordinary traveler journeying from Boston to New York by way of the Lower Road and stopping along the way at various inns and taverns for refreshments, food, and lodgings, might take as much as two weeks to make the trip, provided the weather was balmy. Such a trip in winter would take much longer.

Most of the time, the Colonial peddler traveled on his own two feet. Except for the Boston Post Road and a few other thoroughfares, the only routes he had were those he made himself, or the dim footpaths, old Indian trails, or rivers, streams,

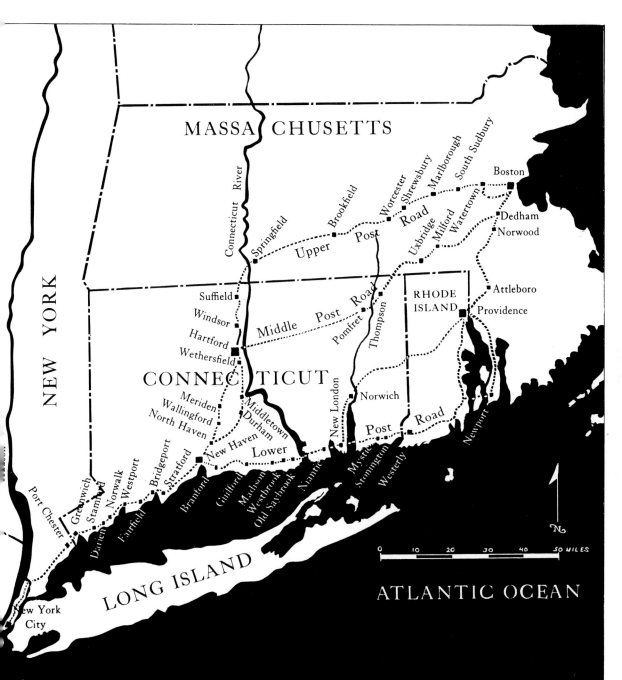

MASSACHUSETTS

NEW YORK

CONNECTICUT

Connecticut River

Springfield

Upper   Post   Road

Brookfield

Worcester

Shrewsbury

Marlborough

South Sudbury

Boston

Dedham

Norwood

Uxbridge

Milford

Watertown

Suffield

Windsor

Hartford

Wethersfield

Middle   Post   Road

Pomfret

Thompson

RHODE
ISLAND

Attleboro

Providence

Meriden

Wallingford

North Haven

Middletown

Durham

New London

Norwich

Newport

New Haven

Lower   Post   Road

Branford

Guilford

Madison

Westbrook

Old Saybrook

Niantic

Mystic

Stonington

Westerly

Greenwich

Stamford

Darien

Norwalk

Westport

Fairfield

Bridgeport

Stratford

Port Chester

New York
City

LONG ISLAND

ATLANTIC OCEAN

N

0   10   20   30   40   50 MILES

THE POST ROAD
IN COLONIAL AMERICA

(The state boundaries are modern ones)

and lakes he might find as he journeyed.

In many instances, the only way by which a peddler could reach an outlying farm or village was by water. A man working out of the Connecticut colony of Saybrook, at the mouth of the Connecticut River, for example, could load his goods onto a raft, and pole upstream. By this means, he could reach people who were hard to get to overland.

The rivers, streams, and lakes were the best and most easily traveled inland roads the colonists had. When a peddler approached a settlement, he blew a bugle to let everyone know that he was coming. From time to time he was able to sell all his goods to the first customer he met. When this happened he immediately went back downriver to load a fresh supply of wares onto his raft.

Because the demand for every kind of article was growing rapidly, many peddlers were able to specialize in one item only, after a while.

There were book peddlers, dealing mostly in religious works. The Book of Psalms and the New Testament were widely sold, as was *The New England Primer*, the Puritans' much used reader

for the very young.

One man in Massachusetts specialized in making horn combs and selling them.

Other peddlers sold dyes. In Colonial days many women did their own spinning and weaving, and the indigo plant was used to color yarn blue. Some wild plants were gathered to make a few other dyes. Certain peddlers carried a stock of all the colors that could be had.

In 1738, Edward and William Pattison of Berlin, Connecticut, began making tinware — dishes, candlesticks, lanterns, and other objects made of thin sheet iron covered with a shiny coating of tin. Almost overnight their tinware became popular. The Pattisons peddled their product all over the countryside around them. Soon they could not make tinware fast enough to supply the people who wanted to buy it. Now they hired more workmen to help them, and instead of peddling their own products they let other men sell them wherever they could. In no time at all, droves of Connecticut Yankees, loaded down with the Pattison brothers' tinware and other useful objects, marched out of their colony in an almost endless

line. They headed for every corner of America where there were people — north, south, east, and west.

Working their way south, the salesmen from Connecticut tracked down every house from New York to the coast of Georgia. The prices of the peddlers were high, but if anyone argued about the cost, they usually blamed the King of England. Or else they blamed the men from whom they had purchased their stock in the first place.

Because they were shrewd and drove a hard bargain, many of the Connecticut Yankee peddlers were not liked in the southern colonies. Still, in the sparsely settled regions of the South, the colonists put up with the northern peddlers. After all, these men did have goods that were needed and that the settlers could not get otherwise. Once in a while, it is true, the southerners became so indignant over the prices charged by a greedy peddler that they tarred and feathered him and chased him to a fast start on his way back to New England.

But the peddlers were not easily discouraged. They returned again and again to the places that

were less than friendly. Business was business. If anyone at all could be found who was willing to buy, they were willing to sell, whatever the place and whatever the price — as long as it was high.

For the most part, too, the Colonial peddlers, although their prices were high, were honest men from respectable families. In many out-of-the-way places the arrival of a Yankee peddler was a great event, and the man was greeted with enthusiasm. Often, in remote parts of the country, he stayed overnight in the farmhouse of one of his customers. Not only did he bring the latest goods, but also the latest news and gossip. Because he traveled so widely, he was likely to know everything that was going on over a wide area. The farm men relied on him for reports on politics and business and the state of the crops in other parts of the country. And the farm women, cut off from the social life of the towns, listened eagerly to his remarks on the latest fashions and the latest doings of the fashionable.

In more settled areas, crowds gathered around his trunks to inspect his wares and buy them, and to hear his endless stories. Sometimes the ped-

dlers were better actors than they were salesmen — or perhaps they were good salesmen because they were good actors. Very often their audiences were so enchanted by their tales that they never realized how high the prices were. In fact, not only did people willingly buy whatever they needed, but they also gave orders to the peddler, to be filled on his next trip to the neighborhood.

During most of the Colonial period few settlers in places far from cities had money with which to pay the peddlers for the things they bought. Instead, they bartered. In exchange for the peddlers' goods the buyers gave goods of their own. Usually these payments were made in animal skins, grain, minerals, or any other kind of product that came from the land and that the peddler could carry. By the time the peddler had finished his journey and his bartering, he often found that the load he carried back was heavier than the one he started out with. But usually he did not mind, as on his way home he was able to sell to merchants the things he had collected. Often he made a profit, but there were times, too, when he found that he had been at the wrong end of a bad bargain.

In a great many instances, people who had neither cash nor extra products from the land used lead bullets in paying the peddler. Ammunition was hard to get and was expensive, but many times it meant life itself to the pioneers in wilderness America. A peddler could quickly sell any musket balls he might have.

The British had always reasoned that if too much currency — bullets or coins — were circulated in the colonies, the settlers would be able to trade with whatever nation offered the best prices. England would then have to compete with other countries for goods from her own colonies. The British would have none of this. They firmly believed that the colonies were there to serve the mother country's interests only.

Between 1652 and 1684 — the years in which the Massachusetts mint operated — some of the settlers, at least, did not have to rely much on musket balls for money. But when the mint closed, bullets once more became useful currency in many sections of the colonies.

By the 1770's the colonists were on the road to revolution. They were beginning to realize that

lead musket balls, far from being used as money, might be used in defying the British.

In the midst of the exploding Colonial anger, bitterness, and excitement stood the Yankee peddler. He was only too happy to accept bullets in payment for his goods. If he was an exceptionally greedy man without loyalty to either the rebellious colonists or to England, he sold the musket balls to the highest bidder and made huge profits. If he was sympathetic to the rebel cause but did not wish to get involved in the fight, he peddled his bullets to the Colonials only, but still made a profit. If he was a true patriot, as most of the peddlers were, he gave his entire supply of ammunition to the Colonials at little or no profit to himself.

To most of the Yankee peddlers the rebel cause was the only cause. It was natural for them to think this. After all, freedom was their way of life — freedom from restrictions, freedom to go wherever they pleased, freedom to sell what they pleased to whomever they pleased, and freedom to charge whatever the customer was willing to pay.

For more than a hundred years after the War of Independence, Yankee peddlers continued to

march in increasing numbers across a growing America. Many of them finally settled down in towns far from home, too tired to make another long trip, or wealthy enough to seek new opportunities and adventure on the American frontiers. Some of these peddlers became successful merchants, leaving new generations of ambitious young men to take over the trade of peddling. A number of these former peddlers-turned-merchants established great business houses that are still thriving today.

Whatever the Colonial peddler was, or was called — cheat, rascal, crook, conniver, sweet talker, actor, shrewd businessman, scoundrel, cad, or damnyankee — he was a strong man with a vivid imagination and a willingness to work hard for everything he got. No group of people in America cherished their individual freedom more than the early peddlers. They were vigorous men who flourished at a time when the American colonies, verging on independence, needed persons of strength, imagination, and enterprise to help push back the frontiers and build a mighty nation.

Index